7 Algorithm design and problem solving

1 Identify and describe **three** stages of the program development lifecycle.

1 ....

....

....

....

2 ....

....

....

....

3 ....

....

....

....

2 Abstraction, decomposition and structure diagrams are tools used during the program development lifecycle. Identify the stage of the program development lifecycle where they are used and describe what they are used for.

Abstraction

Stage: ....

Use: ....

....

....

Decomposition

Stage: ....

Use: ....

....

....

Structure diagram

Stage: ....

Use: ....

....

....

3 a Identify **three** of the different items, other than software, that make up a computer system.

1 ....

2 ....

3 ....

b State **three** of the component parts of a computer system.

1 ....

2 ....

3 ....

4 Identify and describe the **three** methods you could use to design and construct a solution to a problem.

1 ....

....

....

....

2 ....

....

....

....

3 ....

....

....

....

WORKBOOK

Endorsed for learner support

Cambridge IGCSE™ and O Level

Computer Science

Algorithms, Programming and Logic

David Watson
Helen Williams

HODDER EDUCATION

Every effort has been made to trace all copyright holders, but if any have been inadvertently overlooked, the Publishers will be pleased to make the necessary arrangements at the first opportunity.

Although every effort has been made to ensure that website addresses are correct at time of going to press, Hodder Education cannot be held responsible for the content of any website mentioned in this book. It is sometimes possible to find a relocated web page by typing in the address of the home page for a website in the URL window of your browser.

Hachette UK's policy is to use papers that are natural, renewable and recyclable products and made from wood grown in well-managed forests and other controlled sources. The logging and manufacturing processes are expected to conform to the environmental regulations of the country of origin.

Orders: please contact Hachette UK Distribution, Hely Hutchinson Centre, Milton Road, Didcot, Oxfordshire, OX11 7HH. Telephone: +44 (0)1235 827827. Email education@hachette.co.uk Lines are open from 9 a.m. to 5 p.m., Monday to Friday. You can also order through our website: www.hoddereducation.com

ISBN: 978 1 3983 1847 2

© David Watson and Helen Williams 2021

First published in 2021 by
Hodder Education
An Hachette UK Company
Carmelite House
50 Victoria Embankment
London EC4Y 0DZ

www.hoddereducation.com

Impression number   10 9 8 7 6 5 4

Year   2025 2024 2023

Cover © phonlamaiphoto – stock.adobe.com

Typeset in India by Aptara Inc.

Printed in the UK

A catalogue record for this title is available from the British Library.

Contents

Introduction   4

7   Algorithm design and problem solving   5

8   Programming   26

9   Databases   55

10   Boolean logic   63

Introduction

Welcome to the *Cambridge IGCSE™ and O Level Computer Science Algorithms, Programming and Logic Workbook*. This and the companion *Computer Systems Workbook* replace the previous *Computer Science Workbook* and are designed to complement the second edition of the Student's Book and support the Cambridge IGCSE, IGCSE (9-1) and O Level Computer Science syllabuses (0478/0984/2210).

The aim of this Workbook is to provide you with further opportunity to practise the skills and test the knowledge and understanding you have acquired through using Chapters 7 to 10 of the *Cambridge IGCSE and O Level Computer Science Student's Book Second Edition*. It is designed as a 'write-in' book to supplement your learning of different topics as you work through each chapter of the Student's Book and can be used either for home study or in class. The chapters in this Workbook have the same names as those in the Student's Book and reflect the practical topics in the Student's Book.

You are recommended to ensure that all your answers to programming questions work correctly by writing and testing a complete program for each answer. You can then include a copy of your working program in the answer space provided. This enables the completed workbook to be used for revision in preparation for the examination.

If you are working from home using your own computer, you will need to download a free integrated development environment (IDE) for your chosen programming language to write and test your programs. Instructions on how to obtain and use these freely available IDEs are given at the start of Chapter 9.

5 Use the following list of words and phrases to complete the paragraph below.

Each word or phrase can be used once, more than once or not at all.
- breakdown
- bottom-up
- composition
- decomposition
- description
- diagrammatic
- flowchart
- formal
- hierarchical
- level
- program
- pseudocode
- top-down
- structure diagram
- system
- sub-systems

Structure diagrams are used to show the ………………………… design of a computer …………………………

in a ………………………… form.

A structure diagram shows the design of a computer program in a ………………………… way

with each ………………………… giving a more detailed ………………………… of the …………………………

into …………………………

6 a Draw and describe the use of **four** flowchart symbols.

1

……

……

2

……

……

3

……

……

4

....

....

b Describe the purpose of flow lines in a flowchart.

....

....

7 Describe the function of each of the following types of pseudocode statement and give an example in pseudocode of the use of each one.

Assignment:

....

....

....

....

....

Conditional:

....

....

....

....

....

Iterative:

....

....

....

....

....

....

8 a There are **three** different types of loop structure in pseudocode.

For each one, describe the structure and write the pseudocode statements needed to output the names of 20 students that have been stored in the array Student[0:19]. Use the variable Counter for the iteration.

Loop 1: ....

....

....

....

....

....

....

Loop 2: ....

....

....

....

....

....

....

Loop 3: ....

....

....

....

....

....

....

b i There are two different types of conditional statements used in pseudocode.

For each one, write the pseudocode statements needed to output a different welcome message for each name input from 'Alice', 'Abid', 'Dinesh', 'Daisy' or 'Zak' or a rejection message. Use the variable Name for the input.

Conditional Statements 1: ....

....

....

....

....

....

....

....

....

....

....

....

....

....

....

....

....

....

....

....

....

....

....

Conditional Statements 2: ....

....

....

....

....

....

....

....

....

    ii State, with reasons, which conditional statement is more appropriate to use in this case.

....

....

....

c There are **two** different ways of writing a flowchart to output the names of twenty students that have been stored in the array Student[0:19]. The loop counter Counter is tested at the start of the loop (pre-condition) or at the end of the loop (post-condition).

    i Draw flowcharts for the pre-condition loop and the post-condition loop.

Pre-condition loop:

Post-condition loop:

ii Identify which pseudocode loop statements matches each flowchart.

....

....

....

....

d When you have learnt how to write programs that include loops, write three programs to test that your answers to part **a** work as intended.
Hint: for Python there will only be two programs.

Loop 1: ....

....

....

....

....

....

Loop 2: ....

....

....

....

....

Loop 3: ....

....

....

....

....

9 a Write an algorithm in pseudocode to input ten numbers and output the total.

....

....

....

....

....

....

....

....

....

b Write an algorithm using a flowchart to input ten numbers and output the total.

10 Look at this algorithm, shown as a flowchart:

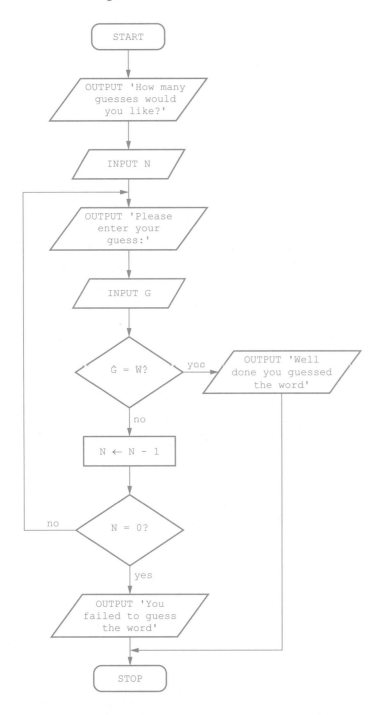

a Identify the processes in the algorithm.

....

....

....

....

....

b Describe the purpose of the algorithm.

....

....

....

....

c Rewrite the algorithm in pseudocode.

....

....

....

....

....

....

....

....

....

....

....

....

....

....

11 Use the following list of words and phrases to complete the paragraph below.

Each word or phrase can be used once, more than once or not at all.

» algorithms   » maximum
» average   » mode
» bubble   » minimum
» counter   » search
» counting   » sort
» linear   » testing
» list   » totalling

Standard methods of solution are used in the design of .... These include

adding in a new value every time an action occurs, for example, awarding a mark to each

student – this is called .... When divided by the number of times this

occurs, this gives the .... Keeping a record of the number of times an

action occurs is called .... Finding the largest, ... ,

and smallest, ... , are also standard methods.

In order to look for an item in a list a .... is used. The method you need to

know for IGCSE Computer Science is to inspect each item in the .... in turn to

see if it is the one required. This is called a ....

To put a list in order a .... is used. The method you need to know for IGCSE

Computer Science is called a ....

12 a Explain the operation of a bubble sort.

....

....

....

....

b Write a bubble sort algorithm in pseudocode to sort a list of ten names, in an array called Names[], in ascending order.

....

....

....

....

....

....

....

....

13 Validation and verification checks are used on values that are input into a computer program.

a i State when it is appropriate to use validation.

....

....

ii State when it is appropriate to use verification.

....

....

b i Give **two** examples of validation checks.

1 ....

2 ....

ii Give **two** examples of verification checks.

1 ....

2 ....

14 a Explain the purpose of test data.

....

....

....

....

b i Boundary data is one type of test data. Identify and describe **three** other types of test data.

1 ....

....

....

....

2 ....

....

....

....

3 ....

....

....

....

ii Give the set of boundary data needed to check that a whole number is less than 100.

1 ....

2 ....

15 a Use the trace table and the test data 78, 34, 22, −4, 98, 16, 734, 88, 999 to record a dry run of this algorithm written in pseudocode.

```
W ← 0
X ← 0
Y ← 100
Z ← 0
REPEAT
    INPUT Mark
    IF Mark <> 999
      THEN
        REPEAT
            IF Mark < 0 OR Mark > 100
              THEN
                  INPUT Mark
            ENDIF
        UNTIL Mark >= 0 AND Mark <= 100
        IF Mark > X
          THEN
            X ← Mark
        ENDIF
        IF Mark < Y
          THEN
            Y ← Mark
        ENDIF
        Z ← Z + Mark
        W ← W + 1
    ENDIF
UNTIL Mark = 999
OUTPUT X, Y, Z
```

W	X	Y	Z	Mark	OUTPUT

b State the purpose of the algorithm.

....

....

....

....

c Rewrite the algorithm as a flowchart.

d Use the guidance in Chapter 8 to rewrite this algorithm in pseudocode, ensuring that:
  » there are meaningful prompts and outputs
  » the algorithm could be read and understood by someone else.

....

....

....

....

....

....

....

....

....

....

....

....

....

....

....

....

....

....

e Devise another set of test data that includes normal, erroneous and extreme data and complete a trace table to perform a dry run on your algorithm.

Test data: ....

....

Trace table:

16 The following flowchart shows an algorithm that checks a temperature input is between 20 and 30 degrees. It contains several errors.

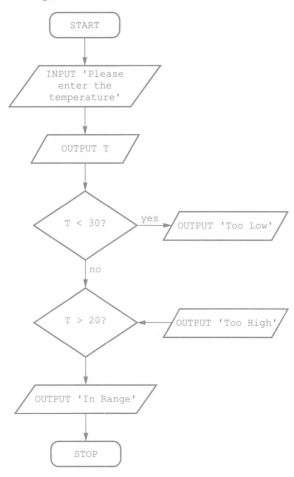

a Identify the errors in the algorithm and the flowchart construction.

....

....

....

....

....

....

....

....

....

b Draw the corrected flowchart.

8 Programming

Before starting to program, you must choose your programming language (tick when complete). ☐

My choice of programming language is: ....

The integrated development environment (IDE)

If your school computers already have an integrated development environment (IDE) then you can use that to write your programs. Otherwise you will need to download and install a development environment to use. Here are some suggestions.

Python

https://www.python.org/downloads/

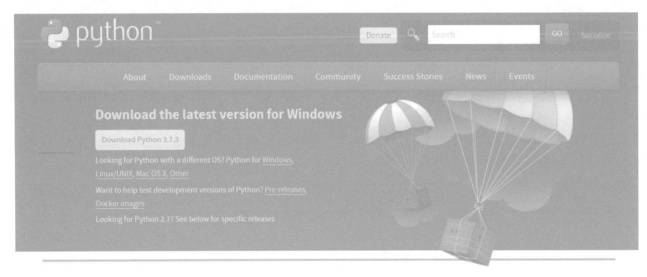

The download is free. Download and install it. The IDE, called IDLE, will provide an editing window:

... and a runtime window:

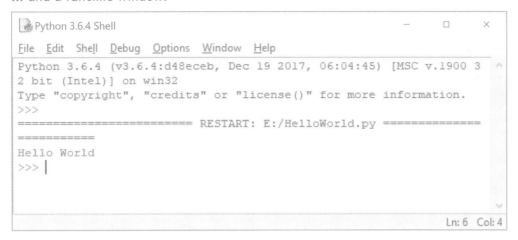

```
Python 3.6.4 Shell                                    —    □    ×
File  Edit  Shell  Debug  Options  Window  Help
Python 3.6.4 (v3.6.4:d48eceb, Dec 19 2017, 06:04:45) [MSC v.1900 3
2 bit (Intel)] on win32
Type "copyright", "credits" or "license()" for more information.
>>>
========================= RESTART: E:/HelloWorld.py ===============
===========
Hello World
>>> |
                                                    Ln: 6   Col: 4
```

Java

https://www.bluej.org/

BlueJ

A free Java Development Environment
designed for beginners, used by millions
worldwide. Find out more...

"One of my favourite IDEs out there is BlueJ"
— James Gosling, creator of Java.

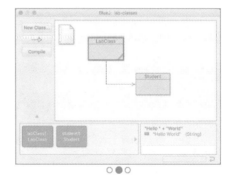

Created by KING'S College LONDON

Supported by ORACLE

Download and Install

Version 4.2.1, released 30 April 2019 (fixes startup freeze, changed-on-disk dialog, and more)

Windows   Mac OS X   Ubuntu/Debian   Other

Download and install. It is free and will provide a project window:

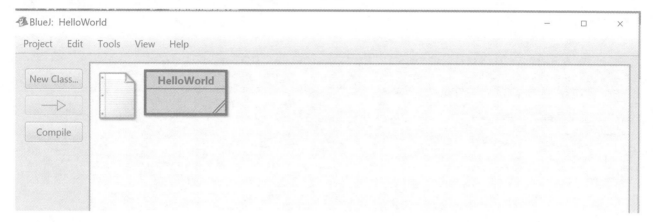

... an editing window:

```java
public class HelloWorld
{
  public static void main(String[] args)
  {
    System.out.println("Hello World");
  }
}
```

... and a terminal window to show the output from the program:

Visual Basic

https://visualstudio.microsoft.com/vs/express/

Download and install the community version. It is free and will provide an editing window:

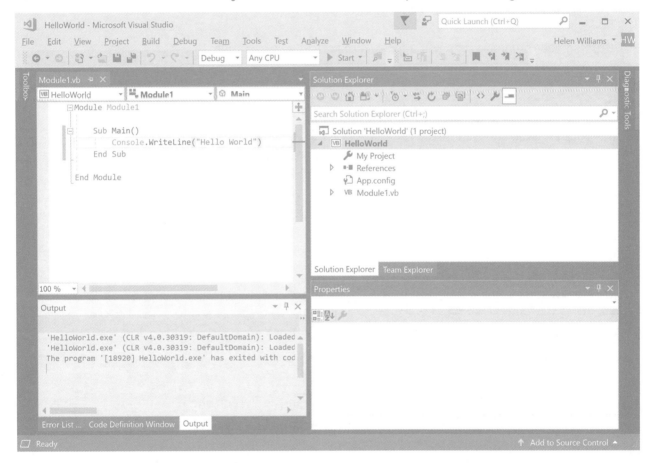

Programs written in console mode, once compiled, run at the command prompt:

Action: download and install the IDE for your chosen programming language (tick when complete). ☐

Now follow the instructions for your chosen programming language to write your first program.

Writing your first program in Python

Click on the IDE Icon to open Python.

Choose **File>New File**.

The editing window will open.

Start typing your program. Help will appear automatically as you type.

To save your program choose **File>Save** or press **Ctrl S**.

To run your program choose **Run>Run Module** or press **F5**.

If there are no syntax errors, then the program will run in the Python shell.

If there are syntax errors, then the IDE will show you where and provide an error message.

Action: write and run a Python program to output Hello World (tick when complete). ☐

Writing your first program in Java

Click on the IDE Icon to open Java.

Choose **Project>New Project**.

Enter the file **Name** and **Location**.

Then click on OK.

Choose **New Class**.

Give the project the **Class Name** HelloWorld. (THIS MUST BE THE SAME NAME AS THE BASE CLASS OF YOUR PROGRAM.)

Choose OK and your new class is constructed.

The class icon appears on the screen.

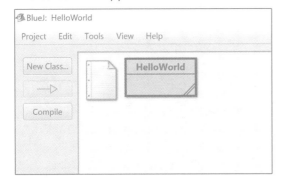

Double click on the icon to edit your program.

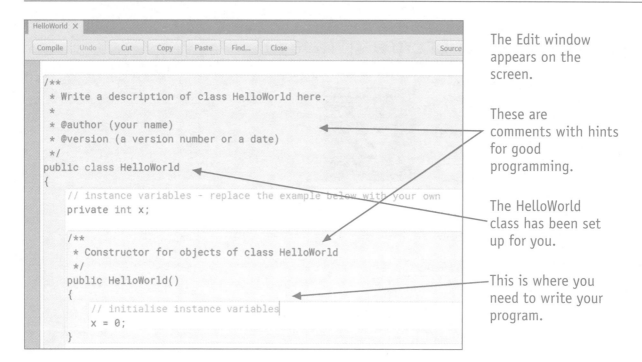

The Edit window appears on the screen.

These are comments with hints for good programming.

The HelloWorld class has been set up for you.

This is where you need to write your program.

Remove any lines not needed.

Type your program.

Once finished, press the **Compile** button.

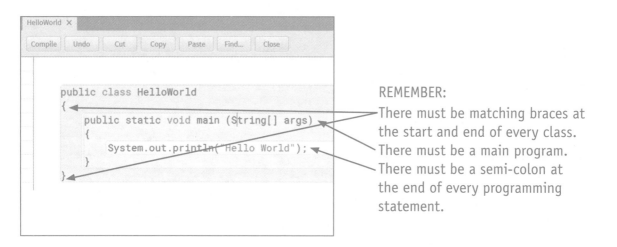

REMEMBER:
There must be matching braces at the start and end of every class.
There must be a main program.
There must be a semi-colon at the end of every programming statement.

If the program has no syntax errors the class icon appears on the screen without any hatching.

 Cambridge IGCSE and O Level Computer Science Algorithms, Programming and Logic Workbook

Right click on the icon then choose **void main(String[] args)**. Then click on OK.

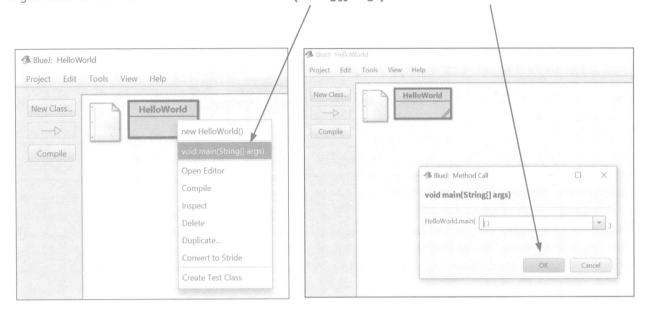

The program will run in a terminal window.

If there are syntax errors, then the IDE will show you where and provide an error message.

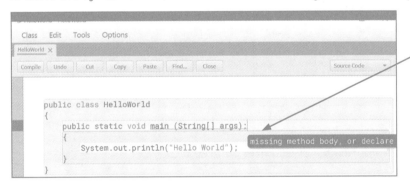

... and the class icon appears on the screen with hatching.

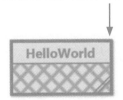

Action: write and run a Java program to output Hello World (tick when complete). ☐

Writing your first program in Visual Basic

Click on the IDE Icon to open Visual Basic.

Choose **File>New>Project>Console App**.

Make sure the language selected is Visual Basic.

Then click on OK.

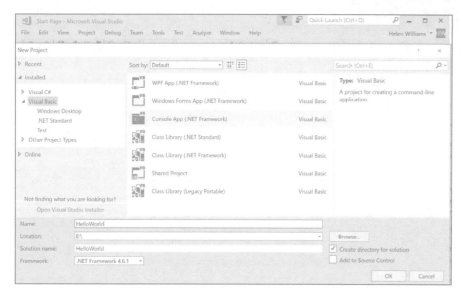

The editing window will appear with a skeleton program ready for you to add your code.

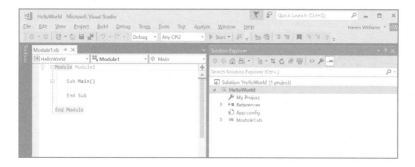

Suggestions will appear to help you write your code. Press **Enter** to accept a highlighted suggestion.

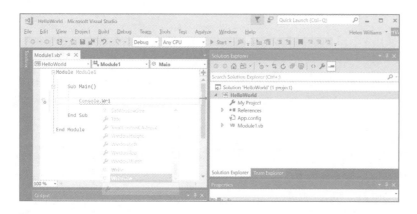

Your program will run in a command line window. The **Console.ReadKey()** will ensure that the output remains on screen.

To run your program press **F5**.

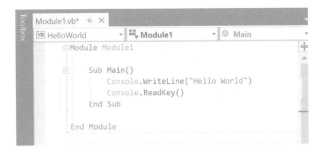

This window will remain on screen until you press a key:

If there are syntax errors, then the IDE will show you where and provide an error message.

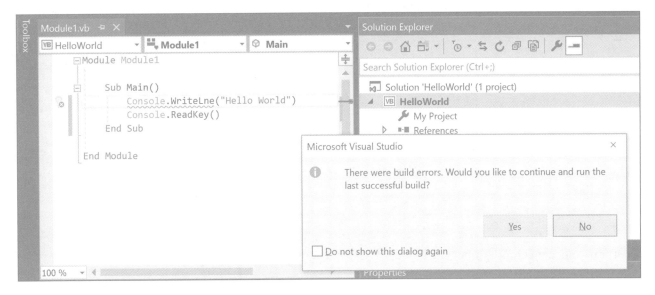

Action: write and run a Visual Basic program to output Hello World (tick when complete). ☐

Getting started

There is plenty of information about getting started using an IDE. Remember you will be writing programs in console mode. Here are some examples.

Python using IDLE

http://web.mit.edu/6.s189/www/handouts/GettingStarted.html

https://sites.physics.utoronto.ca/comp-physics/manual/tutorial-part-1-first-steps-with-idle-and-python

Java using BlueJ

https://www.cs.utexas.edu/~scottm/cs307/handouts/BlueJProjectInstructions.html

http://cs.carleton.edu/faculty/jondich/courses/cs117_w02/labs/lab1.html

Visual Basic using Visual Studio

https://docs.microsoft.com/en-us/visualstudio/ide/quickstart-visual-basic-console?view=vs-2019

https://www.ict.social/vbnet/basics/visual-studio-and-your-first-vbnet-console-application

Action: check out one of the links for your chosen programming language (tick when complete). ☐

Action: find and watch a YouTube video for using your chosen programming language in console mode (tick when complete). ☐

1 Identify and describe **three** basic data types.

1 ....

....

....

2 ....

....

....

3 ....

....

....

2 a In your chosen programming language write a prompt and input statement(s) to enter **three** whole numbers.

....

....

....

....

....

....

b In your chosen programming language write statement(s) to assign the values, 10, 20 and 30 to **three** variables.

....

....

....

c In your chosen programming language write a message and an output statement to display **three** whole numbers that have been stored.

....

....

....

d In your chosen programming language, using your answers to **a**, **b** and **c** above, write and test a program that assigns **three** user-input numbers to **three** variables and displays the values; then assigns numbers to the same three variables and displays the values. You may need to declare the variables used to store your numbers. Write or paste a copy of your program here.

....

....

....

....

....

....

....

....

....

....

....

....

....

3 a In your chosen programming language write a statement to only accept a parcel between 0.5 and 5.0 kilograms.

....

....

....

b In your chosen programming language write a statement to only accept a menu choice that is 1, 2, 3, 4 or 5.

....

....

....

....

....

c In your chosen programming language write and test a program that:

i accepts parcels between 0.5 and 5.0 kilograms in weight

ii displays a menu of options for the cost of sending the parcel

iii calculates and outputs the cost
  - option 1 weight times $10 plus $1
  - option 2 weight times $10
  - option 3 $5
  - option 4 $4
  - option 5 $3

Options	
1	Guaranteed next day delivery before noon
2	Guaranteed next day delivery
3	24-hour delivery
4	48-hour delivery
5	3–5 days delivery

Write or paste a copy of your program here.

....

....

....

....

....

....

d Test your program with the following test data and complete this table.

Test data	Expected output	Actual output
0.4		
5.1		
− 1		
0.5 Option 1		
0.5 Option 2		
0.5 Option 3		
5 Option 1		
5 Option 2		
5 Option 4		
1 Option 5		

4 Describe each program concept and give an example in a programming language.

a Counting:

....

....

....

....

b Iteration:

....

....

....

....

c Selection:

....

....

....

....

d Sequence:

....

....

....

....

e String handling:

....

....

....

....

5 Put the following pseudocode statements in the correct order for this algorithm.
   Make sure that you indent each statement correctly.

```
// Algorithm to input ten positive numbers and total them, output the total and then
// average
A ← 0
A ← A + C
B ← 0
B ← B + 1
D = A / B
DECLARE A, B, C, D : INTEGER
DECLARE D : REAL
INPUT C
OUTPUT A, D
OUTPUT "Please enter a positive number "
REPEAT
REPEAT
UNTIL B = 10
UNTIL C > 0
```

....

....

....

....

....

....

....

....

....

....

....

....

....

....

6 a In your chosen programming language write a program for an improved algorithm for Question **5**. Your program must use:
- » meaningful variable names
- » appropriate prompts and messages
- » relevant comments.

Write or paste a copy of your program here.

....

....

....

....

....

....

....

....

....

....

b Test your program with this test data:

4, 3, 7, 6 ,0, –3, 9, 1, 8, 5, 2, 5

Show your results in this trace table.

7 a Choose two different types of loop structure.

   For each one, write and test a program to output the names of eight students that have been stored in the array Student[0:7]. Use the variable Counter for the iteration.

b Extend one of your programs to work for any number of students, outputting the list of students and number of students in the array.

Write or paste a copy of your program here.

....

....

....

....

....

....

....

....

8 a Write pseudocode statements to perform the following string handling operations on the variable MyString.

Find the length ....

....

Convert to upper case ....

....

Convert to lower case ....

....

Find the first character ....

....

b In your chosen programming language write a program to perform the four string operations from part **a**. Test your program with the string "Test String" stored in the variable MyString. Write or paste a copy of your program here.

....

....

....

....

....

....

....

....

....

....

....

....

....

9 a This pseudocode statement performs a calculation:

```
A ← ((B + C - D * E) ^ F) / G
```

Write this statement in your chosen programming language.

....

....

....

b This pseudocode statement uses a nested IF and performs a logical operation:

```
IF (A = B) OR (C <> D)
  THEN
    A ← 0
  ELSE
    IF (A > B) AND (C = D)
      THEN
        B ← 0
    ENDIF
ENDIF
```

Write this statement in your chosen programming language.

....

....

....

....

....

....

....

....

....

....

....

c Write pseudocode statements to use a nested FOR .. NEXT loop to output the numbers 1 to 10 twenty times.

....

....

....

....

....

....

d Write and test a program to use a nested FOR .. NEXT loop to output the numbers 1 to 10 twenty times. Write or paste a copy of your program here.

....

....

....

....

....

....

....

....

....

....

....

....

....

....

....

10 Use the following list of words and phrases to complete the paragraph below.

Each word can be used once, more than once or not at all.

- » called
- » code
- » constant
- » defined
- » functions
- » global
- » local
- » parameters
- » procedures
- » program
- » return
- » value

Tasks that are repeated many times in an algorithm make use of .... and

.... Use of these can reduce the size of a ....

Procedures and functions are .... once and .... many times.

They can be written with and without .... They are the variables that store the

values passed to a procedure or function.

Functions always .... a .... and the value can be used on

the right-hand side of an assignment statement.

A variable that can be used in any part of a program is called a .... variable.

A variable that is declared within a procedure or function is called a .... variable.

11 a Describe the purpose of a library routine.

....

....

....

....

b Identify **four** library routines that you need to be able to use for IGCSE.

1 ....

2 ....

3 ....

4 ....

c Write and test a program that uses library routines to create two random integers with values between 10 and 20, finds the quotient and remainder of the first integer divided by the second, and outputs all four values with suitable messages. Write or paste a copy of your program here.

....

....

....

....

....

....

....

....

12 a Explain the meaning of the following terminology.

Array: ....

....

Array dimension: ....

....

Array index: ....

....

b Write a procedure in pseudocode to display the contents of a three by three array that stores the current state of a noughts and crosses game. The display should look just like a noughts and crosses game, using 'X's and 'O's on three separate lines.

....

....

....

....

....

....

c Write a program that uses a procedure to display the contents of a three by three array that stores the current state of a noughts and crosses game. Test the program with this data. Each row must start on a new line. Write or paste a copy of your program here.

Here is an example of what might be displayed on screen:

```
O
  X
  X  O
```

....

....

....

....

....

....

....

....

....

....

13 a Explain the purpose of using files to store data.

....

....

....

....

b i Write pseudocode statements to store the word 'Test' in the file 'MyFile.txt'.

....

....

....

....

....

....

ii Write pseudocode statements to read and display the word stored in the file 'MyFile.txt'.

....

....

....

....

....

....

....

c Write a program to store the word 'Test' in the file 'MyFile.txt', then read and display the word stored in the file 'MyFile.txt'. Write or paste a copy of your program here.

....

....

....

....

....

....

....

....

....

....

....

....

14 a Write a program to ask a user if they want to:

1 Enter a new password

2 Check their password

3 Change their password

4 Quit

The program should call an appropriately named procedure or function for each option. It should also include a loop that only stops if option 4 is selected.

Write or paste a copy of your program here.

....

....

....

....

....

....

....

....

b Write a procedure or function for option 1 from the program in part **a** to input a word to use for a password. It should check the following about the word:
  » It is between 10 and 20 characters in length.
  » It does not contain any spaces.
  » It contains at least one uppercase letter.
  » It contains at least one digit between 0 and 9.

The procedure or function should output suitable error messages if the password does not meet each of these conditions. Write or paste a copy of your procedure/function here.

....

....

....

....

....

....

....

....

....

....

Test your program with the following test data and complete this table.

Test data	Expected output	Actual output
Password		
Password99		
password99		
Password99!		
ExtraLargePassword9999999		
2 1		

c   Extend your code from part **b** to store a valid password in the file 'MyPassword.txt'.

Write or paste a copy of the extension to your procedure/function here.

....

....

....

....

....

....

....

....

....

....

....

....

....

....

....

....

....

d Write another procedure or function for option 2 from the program in part **a** to input a password and check that it matches the password stored in 'MyPassword.txt'. Write or paste a copy of your procedure/function here.

....

....

....

....

....

....

....

....

....

....

....

e Write another procedure or function for option 3 from the program in part **a**. It should ask the user to enter the current password and check that this is correct (i.e. matches the one stored in 'MyPassword.txt') before allowing them to change their password. The new password should match all of the requirements of a password listed in part **b**. (HINT: It is possible to call one procedure or function from within another procedure or function.) Write or paste a copy of your procedure/function here.

....

....

....

....

....

....

....

....

....

15 Write and test a program that uses a two-dimensional array, Game[] to store the moves in a noughts and crosses game. The program should meet the following requirements:
  » Start each game with an empty array.
  » Allow two players to input their moves in turn; the contents of the array are displayed before and after every move.
  » One player can input O and the other input X; no other moves are allowed, and no move can use a space in the array already occupied.
  » After every move the program should check for a completed line of three Os or three Xs, and if found output the winner of the game.
  » Use procedures and parameters.
  » Include comments to explain how your code works.

....

....

....

....

....

....

....

....

....

....

....

....

....

....

....

....

....

9 Databases

1 a Explain the meaning of the following database terminology.

Table: ....

....

....

Record: ....

....

....

Field: ....

....

....

b Identify **four** basic data types used in a database and provide an example for each one.

1 ....

....

....

2 ....

....

....

3 ....

....

....

4 ....

....

....

2 A single-table database, ICECREAM, has been set up to store the ice creams available for sale. The details included about each type of ice cream are:
» Type – for example, 'choc ice', 'lolly' or 'cone'
» Flavour – for example, 'raspberry'
» Size – 'Small', 'Medium' or 'Large'
» Number in stock – for example, '34'
» Re-order level – for example, '20'.

a Write down names for the five fields that would be required. For each field state with a reason the data type that should be used and give a sample of the contents of that field.

Field 1: ....

Data type: ....

Reason: ....

....

Sample: ....

Field 2: ....

Data type: ....

Reason: ....

....

Sample: ....

Field 3: ....

Data type: ....

Reason: ....

....

Sample: ....

Field 4: ....

Data type: ....

Reason: ....

....

Sample: ....

Field 5: ....

Data type: ....

Reason: ....

....

Sample: ....

b i Explain why a primary key is needed in a database table.

....

....

....

....

ii Give the reason why none of the existing fields are suitable to use as a primary key.

....

....

iii Give a suitable field name, data type and sample for another field that could be used as a primary key.

Name: ....

Data type: ....

....

Sample: ....

c Build the database table as specified in parts **a** and **b**. Write or paste a copy of your table structure here.

d Populate the database table with **six** records. Write or paste a copy of your populated table here.

3 a Explain what is meant by SQL.

....

....

....

....

b Explain the function of each of the following SQL statements.

i SELECT

....

....

....

....

ii FROM

....

....

iii WHERE

....

....

....

....

iv SUM

....

....

....

....

c Identify **two** more SQL statements that you need to know for IGCSE Computer Science.

1 ....

2 ....

d Use the six statements from parts **b** and **c** to write SQL queries for the database table you created in Question **2** to:
   » Show the types, in alphabetical order, and sizes of all the ice creams that are in stock
   » Show the total number of ice creams available to buy
   » Count the number of ice creams that have stock below the reorder level.

Write or paste a copy of your SQL queries here.

....

....

....

....

....

....

....

....

....

4 A single-table database, TEACHER, contains the details of the teachers in a school. The database includes these fields:

Name – the teacher's family name, for example, 'Yo'

Title – the teacher's title, for example, 'Mr'

Licence – the teacher's licence number, for example, 'L1234'

Gender – 'M' or 'F'

Subject – the main subject taught by the teacher, for example, 'Mathematics'

Class – the class the teacher tutors, for example, '2Y'

a i Identify the field that would be most suitable to use as a primary key. Give a reason for your choice.

....

....

....

....

ii State the data type that could be used for each field.

Name: ....

Title: ....

Licence: ....

Gender: ....

Subject: ....

Class: ....

iii Build a database with the six records shown.

b i Identify a field that should be verified. Give a reason for your choice.

....

....

....

....

ii Identify a field that could be validated. Give a reason for your choice.

....

....

....

....

iii Add your validation to your database.

Here is part of the database table, TEACHER:

Name	Title	Licence	Gender	Subject	Class
Yo	Mr	L4579	M	Mathematics	3Z
Sing	Miss	L6713	F	Science	2X
Patel	Mr	L5421	M	Geography	4Y
Tco	Mrs	L7681	F	Mathematics	2Z
Young	Mrs	L6789	F	English	3X
Ling	Mr	L4980	M	Science	4X

c i State the output from this SQL query.

SELECT Title, Name

FROM TEACHER

WHERE Subject = 'Science';

....

....

....

ii Add the SQL statement to show the results in alphabetical order.

....

....

....

iii Rewrite this SQL statement to include the mathematics teachers as well.

....

....

iv Write a new SQL statement to count the number of mathematics teachers in the TEACHER table.

v Check that the SQL statements work for your database.

d Write an SQL statement to display the names of all the teachers and their classes in ascending order of class.

....

....

....

....

....

....

....

....

Check that your SQL statement works as expected.

10 Boolean logic

1 State the logic gate each truth table represents.

a

A	B	X
0	0	0
0	1	1
1	0	1
1	1	1

....

b

A	B	X
0	0	1
0	1	1
1	0	1
1	1	0

....

c

A	B	X
0	0	0
0	1	1
1	0	1
1	1	0

....

2 Complete the truth table for this logic circuit.

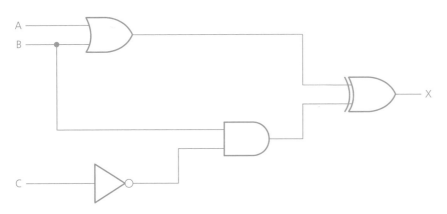

A	B	C	Working area	X
0	0	0		
0	0	1		
0	1	0		
0	1	1		
1	0	0		
1	0	1		
1	1	0		
1	1	1		

3 a Write the following statement as a logic expression:

X is 1 if A and B are on or if B is off and C is on

....

....

b Draw the logic circuit to represent the statement in part **a**.

4 a Complete the truth table for the following logic circuit:

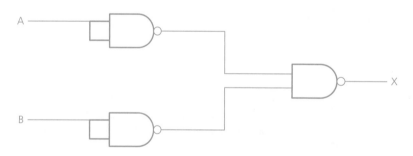

A	B	Working area	X
0	0		
0	1		
1	0		
1	1		

b Which single logic gate is represented by the truth table in part **a**?

....

5 a Complete the truth table for the following logic circuit:

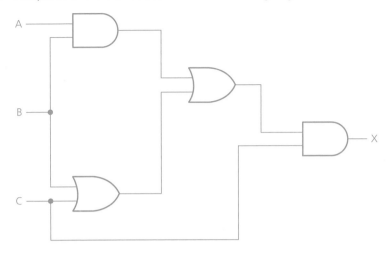

A	B	C	Working area	X
0	0	0		
0	0	1		
0	1	0		
0	1	1		
1	0	0		
1	0	1		
1	1	0		
1	1	1		

b How might the logic circuit in part **a** be simplified?

....

....

6 a Complete the truth table for this logic circuit:

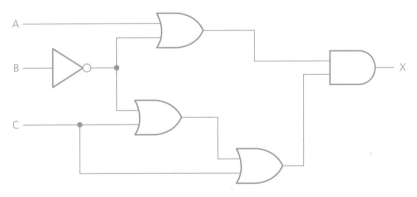

A	B	C	Working area	X
0	0	0		
0	0	1		
0	1	0		
0	1	1		
1	0	0		
1	0	1		
1	1	0		
1	1	1		

b What single logic gate could replace this logic circuit?

....

7 a Write down the logic expression to represent the following logic circuit:

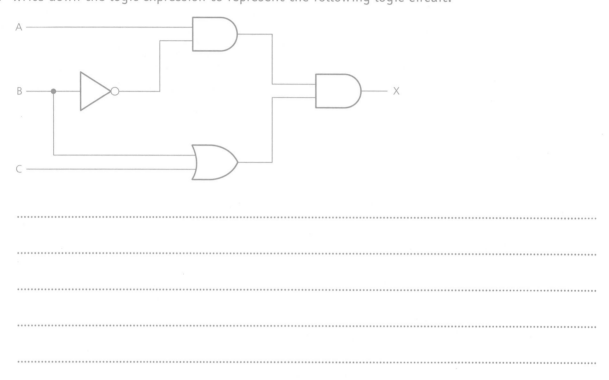

....

....

....

....

....

b Draw the logic circuit which corresponds to the following truth table:

A	B	C	X
0	0	0	1
0	0	1	0
0	1	0	1
0	1	1	1
1	0	0	1
1	0	1	0
1	1	0	1
1	1	1	1

8 A chemical process is monitored using a logic circuit. There are three inputs to the logic circuit representing the parameters being monitored in the chemical process. An alarm, X, will give an output value of 1 depending on certain conditions.

The following table describes the process conditions being monitored.

Parameter description	Parameter	Binary value	Description of condition
Reaction temperature	T	0	Temperature > 120 °C
		1	Temperature <= 120 °C
Pressure of CO gas evolved	P	0	Pressure > 2 bars
		1	Pressure <= 2 bars
Acid concentration	A	0	Acid concentration > 4 moles
		1	Acid concentration <= 4 moles

An alarm, X, will generate the value 1 if:

either   temperature > 120 °C and acid concentration <= 4 moles

or   temperature <= 120 °C and gas pressure <= 2 bars

or   acid concentration > 4 moles and gas pressure <= 2 bars

a Write the logic expression to represent the above system.

....

....

....

....

....

b Draw the logic circuit to represent the above system.

c Complete the truth table to represent the above system.

T	A	P	Working area	X
0	0	0		
0	0	1		
0	1	0		
0	1	1		
1	0	0		
1	0	1		
1	1	0		
1	1	1		

9 A safety system uses the input from three sensors A, B and C. The binary values from these sensors form the input to a logic circuit.

The output, X, from the logic circuit is 1 if:

either   A is 1 and B is 1

or   A is 0 and C is 1

or   B is 0 and C is 1

a Draw the logic circuit to represent the above system.

b Complete the truth table for the above system.

A	B	C	Working area	X
0	0	0		
0	0	1		
0	1	0		
0	1	1		
1	0	0		
1	0	1		
1	1	0		
1	1	1		

c For safety reasons, the sensors feed into three different logic circuits (numbered 1, 2 and 3) which produce the outputs X, Y and Z. These three outputs then form the inputs to another logic circuit which has the output Q.

The three logic circuits are connected to this extra logic circuit:

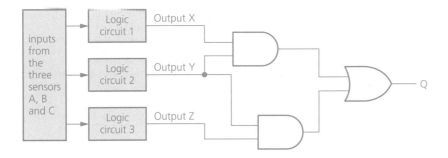

Complete the truth table for this system.

X	Y	Z	Working area	Q
0	0	0		
0	0	1		
0	1	0		
0	1	1		
1	0	0		
1	0	1		
1	1	0		
1	1	1		

10 a Write a logic expression for the following logic circuit:

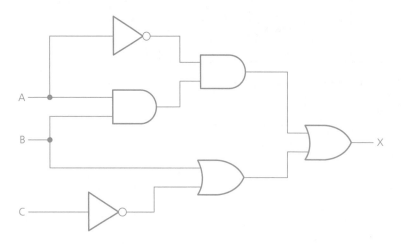

b Complete the truth table for the logic circuit.

A	B	C	Working area	X
0	0	0		
0	0	1		
0	1	0		
0	1	1		
1	0	0		
1	0	1		
1	1	0		
1	1	1		

11 a Write the logic expression for this truth table.

A	B	X
0	0	1
0	1	0
1	0	0
1	1	1

b Draw the logic circuit which is represented by the truth table.

12 a Draw a logic circuit for this logic expression. Each logic gate must have a maximum of **two** inputs and the expression must not be simplified:

X = ((A NAND B) XOR C) OR (A NOR NOT C)

b Complete the truth table for the logic expression:

A	B	C	Working area	X
0	0	0		
0	0	1		
0	1	0		
0	1	1		
1	0	0		
1	0	1		
1	1	0		
1	1	1		

Develop understanding of algorithmic and computational thinking and programming skills with further questions and activities.

This Workbook provides additional support for the Algorithms, Programming and Logic section of the Cambridge IGCSE™ and O Level Computer Science Student's Book Second Edition.

» **Become accomplished computer scientists:** the workbook provides a series of questions designed to test and develop computational thinking skills in order to solve problems.

» **Develop understanding and build confidence:** provides additional practice for use at home or in class throughout the course.

Use with *Cambridge IGCSE™ and O Level Computer Science Student's Book Second Edition*
9781398318281

For over 30 years we have been trusted by Cambridge schools around the world to provide quality support for teaching and learning. For this reason we have been selected by Cambridge Assessment International Education as an official publisher of endorsed material for their syllabuses.

This resource is endorsed by Cambridge Assessment International Education

✓ Provides learner support for the Cambridge IGCSE, IGCSE (9-1) and O Level Computer Science syllabuses (0478/0984/2210) for examination from 2023

✓ Has passed Cambridge International's rigorous quality-assurance process

✓ Developed by subject experts

✓ For Cambridge schools worldwide

HODDER EDUCATION
e: education@hachette.co.uk
w: hoddereducation.com

WORLD LAND TRUST™
www.carbonbalancedprint.com

ISBN 978-1-398-31847-2

9 781398 318472

MIX
Paper | Supporting responsible forestry
FSC™ C10474